I0056741

NAME: _____ **WEEK:** _____ **MONTH:** _____ ~~YEAR:~~ _____

DATE		TIME IN	TIME OUT	BREAKS	OVERTIME	TOTAL
MONDAY						
TUESDAY						
WEDNESDAY						
THURSDAY						
FRIDAY						
SATURDAY						
SUNDAY						
TOTAL HOURS						

NOTES : _____

_____

NAME: _____ **WEEK:** _____ **MONTH:** _____ **YEAR:** _____

DATE		TIME IN	TIME OUT	BREAKS	OVERTIME	TOTAL
MONDAY						
TUESDAY						
WEDNESDAY						
THURSDAY						
FRIDAY						
SATURDAY						
SUNDAY						
TOTAL HOURS						

NOTES : _____

_____

NAME: _____ WEEK: _____ MONTH: _____ YEAR: _____

DATE		TIME IN	TIME OUT	BREAKS	OVERTIME	TOTAL
MONDAY						
TUESDAY						
WEDNESDAY						
THURSDAY						
FRIDAY						
SATURDAY						
SUNDAY						
TOTAL HOURS						

NOTES : _____

_____

NAME: _____ WEEK: _____ MONTH: _____ YEAR: _____

DATE		TIME IN	TIME OUT	BREAKS	OVERTIME	TOTAL
MONDAY						
TUESDAY						
WEDNESDAY						
THURSDAY						
FRIDAY						
SATURDAY						
SUNDAY						
TOTAL HOURS						

NOTES : _____

_____

NAME: _____ WEEK: _____ MONTH: _____ YEAR: _____

DATE		TIME IN	TIME OUT	BREAKS	OVERTIME	TOTAL
MONDAY						
TUESDAY						
WEDNESDAY						
THURSDAY						
FRIDAY						
SATURDAY						
SUNDAY						
TOTAL HOURS						

NOTES : _____

_____

NAME: _____ WEEK: _____ MONTH: _____ YEAR: _____

DATE		TIME IN	TIME OUT	BREAKS	OVERTIME	TOTAL
MONDAY						
TUESDAY						
WEDNESDAY						
THURSDAY						
FRIDAY						
SATURDAY						
SUNDAY						
TOTAL HOURS						

NOTES : _____

_____

NAME: _____ WEEK: _____ MONTH: _____ YEAR: _____

DATE		TIME IN	TIME OUT	BREAKS	OVERTIME	TOTAL
MONDAY						
TUESDAY						
WEDNESDAY						
THURSDAY						
FRIDAY						
SATURDAY						
SUNDAY						
TOTAL HOURS						

NOTES : _____

_____

NAME: _____ WEEK: _____ MONTH: _____ YEAR: _____

DATE		TIME IN	TIME OUT	BREAKS	OVERTIME	TOTAL
MONDAY						
TUESDAY						
WEDNESDAY						
THURSDAY						
FRIDAY						
SATURDAY						
SUNDAY						
TOTAL HOURS						

NOTES : _____

_____

NAME: _____ WEEK: _____ MONTH: _____ YEAR: _____

DATE		TIME IN	TIME OUT	BREAKS	OVERTIME	TOTAL
MONDAY						
TUESDAY						
WEDNESDAY						
THURSDAY						
FRIDAY						
SATURDAY						
SUNDAY						
TOTAL HOURS						

NOTES : _____

_____

NAME: _____ WEEK: _____ MONTH: _____ YEAR: _____

DATE		TIME IN	TIME OUT	BREAKS	OVERTIME	TOTAL
MONDAY						
TUESDAY						
WEDNESDAY						
THURSDAY						
FRIDAY						
SATURDAY						
SUNDAY						
TOTAL HOURS						

NOTES : _____

_____

NAME: _____ WEEK: _____ MONTH: _____ YEAR: _____

DATE		TIME IN	TIME OUT	BREAKS	OVERTIME	TOTAL
MONDAY						
TUESDAY						
WEDNESDAY						
THURSDAY						
FRIDAY						
SATURDAY						
SUNDAY						
TOTAL HOURS						

NOTES : _____

_____

NAME: _____ WEEK: _____ MONTH: _____ YEAR: _____

DATE		TIME IN	TIME OUT	BREAKS	OVERTIME	TOTAL
MONDAY						
TUESDAY						
WEDNESDAY						
THURSDAY						
FRIDAY						
SATURDAY						
SUNDAY						
TOTAL HOURS						

NOTES : _____

_____

NAME: _____ WEEK: _____ MONTH: _____ YEAR: _____

DATE		TIME IN	TIME OUT	BREAKS	OVERTIME	TOTAL
MONDAY						
TUESDAY						
WEDNESDAY						
THURSDAY						
FRIDAY						
SATURDAY						
SUNDAY						
TOTAL HOURS						

NOTES : _____

_____

NAME: _____ WEEK: _____ MONTH: _____ YEAR: _____

DATE		TIME IN	TIME OUT	BREAKS	OVERTIME	TOTAL
MONDAY						
TUESDAY						
WEDNESDAY						
THURSDAY						
FRIDAY						
SATURDAY						
SUNDAY						
TOTAL HOURS						

NOTES : _____

_____

NAME: _____ WEEK: _____ MONTH: _____ YEAR: _____

DATE		TIME IN	TIME OUT	BREAKS	OVERTIME	TOTAL
MONDAY						
TUESDAY						
WEDNESDAY						
THURSDAY						
FRIDAY						
SATURDAY						
SUNDAY						
TOTAL HOURS						

NOTES : _____

_____

NAME: _____ WEEK: _____ MONTH: _____ YEAR: _____

DATE		TIME IN	TIME OUT	BREAKS	OVERTIME	TOTAL
MONDAY						
TUESDAY						
WEDNESDAY						
THURSDAY						
FRIDAY						
SATURDAY						
SUNDAY						
TOTAL HOURS						

NOTES : _____

_____

NAME: _____ WEEK: _____ MONTH: _____ YEAR: _____

DATE		TIME IN	TIME OUT	BREAKS	OVERTIME	TOTAL
MONDAY						
TUESDAY						
WEDNESDAY						
THURSDAY						
FRIDAY						
SATURDAY						
SUNDAY						
TOTAL HOURS						

NOTES : _____

_____

NAME: _____ WEEK: _____ MONTH: _____ YEAR: _____

DATE		TIME IN	TIME OUT	BREAKS	OVERTIME	TOTAL
MONDAY						
TUESDAY						
WEDNESDAY						
THURSDAY						
FRIDAY						
SATURDAY						
SUNDAY						
TOTAL HOURS						

NOTES : _____

_____

NAME: _____ WEEK: _____ MONTH: _____ YEAR: _____

DATE		TIME IN	TIME OUT	BREAKS	OVERTIME	TOTAL
MONDAY						
TUESDAY						
WEDNESDAY						
THURSDAY						
FRIDAY						
SATURDAY						
SUNDAY						
TOTAL HOURS						

NOTES : _____

_____

NAME: _____ WEEK: _____ MONTH: _____ YEAR: _____

DATE		TIME IN	TIME OUT	BREAKS	OVERTIME	TOTAL
MONDAY						
TUESDAY						
WEDNESDAY						
THURSDAY						
FRIDAY						
SATURDAY						
SUNDAY						
TOTAL HOURS						

NOTES : _____

_____

NAME: _____ WEEK: _____ MONTH: _____ YEAR: _____

DATE		TIME IN	TIME OUT	BREAKS	OVERTIME	TOTAL
MONDAY						
TUESDAY						
WEDNESDAY						
THURSDAY						
FRIDAY						
SATURDAY						
SUNDAY						
TOTAL HOURS						

NOTES : _____
_____

NAME: _____ WEEK: _____ MONTH: _____ YEAR: _____

DATE		TIME IN	TIME OUT	BREAKS	OVERTIME	TOTAL
MONDAY						
TUESDAY						
WEDNESDAY						
THURSDAY						
FRIDAY						
SATURDAY						
SUNDAY						
TOTAL HOURS						

NOTES : _____
_____

NAME: _____ WEEK: _____ MONTH: _____ YEAR: _____

DATE		TIME IN	TIME OUT	BREAKS	OVERTIME	TOTAL
MONDAY						
TUESDAY						
WEDNESDAY						
THURSDAY						
FRIDAY						
SATURDAY						
SUNDAY						
TOTAL HOURS						

NOTES : _____

_____

NAME: _____ WEEK: _____ MONTH: _____ YEAR: _____

DATE		TIME IN	TIME OUT	BREAKS	OVERTIME	TOTAL
MONDAY						
TUESDAY						
WEDNESDAY						
THURSDAY						
FRIDAY						
SATURDAY						
SUNDAY						
TOTAL HOURS						

NOTES : _____

_____

NAME: _____ WEEK: _____ MONTH: _____ YEAR: _____

DATE		TIME IN	TIME OUT	BREAKS	OVERTIME	TOTAL
MONDAY						
TUESDAY						
WEDNESDAY						
THURSDAY						
FRIDAY						
SATURDAY						
SUNDAY						
TOTAL HOURS						

NOTES : _____

_____

NAME: _____ WEEK: _____ MONTH: _____ YEAR: _____

DATE		TIME IN	TIME OUT	BREAKS	OVERTIME	TOTAL
MONDAY						
TUESDAY						
WEDNESDAY						
THURSDAY						
FRIDAY						
SATURDAY						
SUNDAY						
TOTAL HOURS						

NOTES : _____

_____

NAME: _____ WEEK: _____ MONTH: _____ YEAR: _____

DATE		TIME IN	TIME OUT	BREAKS	OVERTIME	TOTAL
MONDAY						
TUESDAY						
WEDNESDAY						
THURSDAY						
FRIDAY						
SATURDAY						
SUNDAY						
TOTAL HOURS						

NOTES : _____

_____

NAME: _____ WEEK: _____ MONTH: _____ YEAR: _____

DATE		TIME IN	TIME OUT	BREAKS	OVERTIME	TOTAL
MONDAY						
TUESDAY						
WEDNESDAY						
THURSDAY						
FRIDAY						
SATURDAY						
SUNDAY						
TOTAL HOURS						

NOTES : _____

_____

NAME: _____ WEEK: _____ MONTH: _____ YEAR: _____

DATE		TIME IN	TIME OUT	BREAKS	OVERTIME	TOTAL
MONDAY						
TUESDAY						
WEDNESDAY						
THURSDAY						
FRIDAY						
SATURDAY						
SUNDAY						
TOTAL HOURS						

NOTES : _____

_____

NAME: _____ WEEK: _____ MONTH: _____ YEAR: _____

DATE		TIME IN	TIME OUT	BREAKS	OVERTIME	TOTAL
MONDAY						
TUESDAY						
WEDNESDAY						
THURSDAY						
FRIDAY						
SATURDAY						
SUNDAY						
TOTAL HOURS						

NOTES : _____

_____

NAME: _____ WEEK: _____ MONTH: _____ YEAR: _____

DATE		TIME IN	TIME OUT	BREAKS	OVERTIME	TOTAL
MONDAY						
TUESDAY						
WEDNESDAY						
THURSDAY						
FRIDAY						
SATURDAY						
SUNDAY						
TOTAL HOURS						
NOTES :						

NAME: _____ WEEK: _____ MONTH: _____ YEAR: _____

DATE		TIME IN	TIME OUT	BREAKS	OVERTIME	TOTAL
MONDAY						
TUESDAY						
WEDNESDAY						
THURSDAY						
FRIDAY						
SATURDAY						
SUNDAY						
TOTAL HOURS						
NOTES :						

NAME: _____ WEEK: _____ MONTH: _____ YEAR: _____

DATE		TIME IN	TIME OUT	BREAKS	OVERTIME	TOTAL
MONDAY						
TUESDAY						
WEDNESDAY						
THURSDAY						
FRIDAY						
SATURDAY						
SUNDAY						
TOTAL HOURS						

NOTES : _____
_____

NAME: _____ WEEK: _____ MONTH: _____ YEAR: _____

DATE		TIME IN	TIME OUT	BREAKS	OVERTIME	TOTAL
MONDAY						
TUESDAY						
WEDNESDAY						
THURSDAY						
FRIDAY						
SATURDAY						
SUNDAY						
TOTAL HOURS						

NOTES : _____
_____

NAME: _____ WEEK: _____ MONTH: _____ YEAR: _____

DATE		TIME IN	TIME OUT	BREAKS	OVERTIME	TOTAL
MONDAY						
TUESDAY						
WEDNESDAY						
THURSDAY						
FRIDAY						
SATURDAY						
SUNDAY						
TOTAL HOURS						

NOTES : _____

_____

NAME: _____ WEEK: _____ MONTH: _____ YEAR: _____

DATE		TIME IN	TIME OUT	BREAKS	OVERTIME	TOTAL
MONDAY						
TUESDAY						
WEDNESDAY						
THURSDAY						
FRIDAY						
SATURDAY						
SUNDAY						
TOTAL HOURS						

NOTES : _____

_____

NAME: _____ WEEK: _____ MONTH: _____ YEAR: _____

DATE		TIME IN	TIME OUT	BREAKS	OVERTIME	TOTAL
MONDAY						
TUESDAY						
WEDNESDAY						
THURSDAY						
FRIDAY						
SATURDAY						
SUNDAY						
TOTAL HOURS						

NOTES : _____

_____

NAME: _____ WEEK: _____ MONTH: _____ YEAR: _____

DATE		TIME IN	TIME OUT	BREAKS	OVERTIME	TOTAL
MONDAY						
TUESDAY						
WEDNESDAY						
THURSDAY						
FRIDAY						
SATURDAY						
SUNDAY						
TOTAL HOURS						

NOTES : _____

_____

NAME: _____ WEEK: _____ MONTH: _____ YEAR: _____

DATE		TIME IN	TIME OUT	BREAKS	OVERTIME	TOTAL
MONDAY						
TUESDAY						
WEDNESDAY						
THURSDAY						
FRIDAY						
SATURDAY						
SUNDAY						
TOTAL HOURS						

NOTES : _____

_____

NAME: _____ WEEK: _____ MONTH: _____ YEAR: _____

DATE		TIME IN	TIME OUT	BREAKS	OVERTIME	TOTAL
MONDAY						
TUESDAY						
WEDNESDAY						
THURSDAY						
FRIDAY						
SATURDAY						
SUNDAY						
TOTAL HOURS						

NOTES : _____

_____

NAME: _____ WEEK: _____ MONTH: _____ YEAR: _____

DATE	TIME IN	TIME OUT	BREAKS	OVERTIME	TOTAL
MONDAY					
TUESDAY					
WEDNESDAY					
THURSDAY					
FRIDAY					
SATURDAY					
SUNDAY					
TOTAL HOURS					

NOTES : _____

_____

NAME: _____ WEEK: _____ MONTH: _____ YEAR: _____

DATE	TIME IN	TIME OUT	BREAKS	OVERTIME	TOTAL
MONDAY					
TUESDAY					
WEDNESDAY					
THURSDAY					
FRIDAY					
SATURDAY					
SUNDAY					
TOTAL HOURS					

NOTES : _____

_____

NAME: _____ WEEK: _____ MONTH: _____ YEAR: _____

DATE		TIME IN	TIME OUT	BREAKS	OVERTIME	TOTAL
MONDAY						
TUESDAY						
WEDNESDAY						
THURSDAY						
FRIDAY						
SATURDAY						
SUNDAY						
TOTAL HOURS						

NOTES : _____

_____

NAME: _____ WEEK: _____ MONTH: _____ YEAR: _____

DATE		TIME IN	TIME OUT	BREAKS	OVERTIME	TOTAL
MONDAY						
TUESDAY						
WEDNESDAY						
THURSDAY						
FRIDAY						
SATURDAY						
SUNDAY						
TOTAL HOURS						

NOTES : _____

_____

NAME: _____ WEEK: _____ MONTH: _____ YEAR: _____

DATE		TIME IN	TIME OUT	BREAKS	OVERTIME	TOTAL
MONDAY						
TUESDAY						
WEDNESDAY						
THURSDAY						
FRIDAY						
SATURDAY						
SUNDAY						
TOTAL HOURS						

NOTES : _____

_____

NAME: _____ WEEK: _____ MONTH: _____ YEAR: _____

DATE		TIME IN	TIME OUT	BREAKS	OVERTIME	TOTAL
MONDAY						
TUESDAY						
WEDNESDAY						
THURSDAY						
FRIDAY						
SATURDAY						
SUNDAY						
TOTAL HOURS						

NOTES : _____

_____

NAME: _____ WEEK: _____ MONTH: _____ YEAR: _____

DATE		TIME IN	TIME OUT	BREAKS	OVERTIME	TOTAL
MONDAY						
TUESDAY						
WEDNESDAY						
THURSDAY						
FRIDAY						
SATURDAY						
SUNDAY						
TOTAL HOURS						

NOTES : _____

_____

NAME: _____ WEEK: _____ MONTH: _____ YEAR: _____

DATE		TIME IN	TIME OUT	BREAKS	OVERTIME	TOTAL
MONDAY						
TUESDAY						
WEDNESDAY						
THURSDAY						
FRIDAY						
SATURDAY						
SUNDAY						
TOTAL HOURS						

NOTES : _____

_____

NAME: _____ WEEK: _____ MONTH: _____ YEAR: _____

DATE		TIME IN	TIME OUT	BREAKS	OVERTIME	TOTAL
MONDAY						
TUESDAY						
WEDNESDAY						
THURSDAY						
FRIDAY						
SATURDAY						
SUNDAY						
TOTAL HOURS						

NOTES : _____

_____

NAME: _____ WEEK: _____ MONTH: _____ YEAR: _____

DATE		TIME IN	TIME OUT	BREAKS	OVERTIME	TOTAL
MONDAY						
TUESDAY						
WEDNESDAY						
THURSDAY						
FRIDAY						
SATURDAY						
SUNDAY						
TOTAL HOURS						

NOTES : _____

_____

NAME: _____ WEEK: _____ MONTH: _____ YEAR: _____

DATE		TIME IN	TIME OUT	BREAKS	OVERTIME	TOTAL
MONDAY						
TUESDAY						
WEDNESDAY						
THURSDAY						
FRIDAY						
SATURDAY						
SUNDAY						
TOTAL HOURS						

NOTES : _____

_____

NAME: _____ WEEK: _____ MONTH: _____ YEAR: _____

DATE		TIME IN	TIME OUT	BREAKS	OVERTIME	TOTAL
MONDAY						
TUESDAY						
WEDNESDAY						
THURSDAY						
FRIDAY						
SATURDAY						
SUNDAY						
TOTAL HOURS						

NOTES : _____

_____

NAME: _____ WEEK: _____ MONTH: _____ YEAR: _____

DATE		TIME IN	TIME OUT	BREAKS	OVERTIME	TOTAL
MONDAY						
TUESDAY						
WEDNESDAY						
THURSDAY						
FRIDAY						
SATURDAY						
SUNDAY						
TOTAL HOURS						

NOTES : _____

_____

NAME: _____ WEEK: _____ MONTH: _____ YEAR: _____

DATE		TIME IN	TIME OUT	BREAKS	OVERTIME	TOTAL
MONDAY						
TUESDAY						
WEDNESDAY						
THURSDAY						
FRIDAY						
SATURDAY						
SUNDAY						
TOTAL HOURS						

NOTES : _____

_____

NAME: _____ WEEK: _____ MONTH: _____ YEAR: _____

DATE		TIME IN	TIME OUT	BREAKS	OVERTIME	TOTAL
MONDAY						
TUESDAY						
WEDNESDAY						
THURSDAY						
FRIDAY						
SATURDAY						
SUNDAY						
TOTAL HOURS						

NOTES : _____

_____

NAME: _____ WEEK: _____ MONTH: _____ YEAR: _____

DATE		TIME IN	TIME OUT	BREAKS	OVERTIME	TOTAL
MONDAY						
TUESDAY						
WEDNESDAY						
THURSDAY						
FRIDAY						
SATURDAY						
SUNDAY						
TOTAL HOURS						

NOTES : _____

_____

NAME: _____ WEEK: _____ MONTH: _____ YEAR: _____

DATE	TIME IN	TIME OUT	BREAKS	OVERTIME	TOTAL
MONDAY					
TUESDAY					
WEDNESDAY					
THURSDAY					
FRIDAY					
SATURDAY					
SUNDAY					
TOTAL HOURS					

NOTES : _____

_____

NAME: _____ WEEK: _____ MONTH: _____ YEAR: _____

DATE	TIME IN	TIME OUT	BREAKS	OVERTIME	TOTAL
MONDAY					
TUESDAY					
WEDNESDAY					
THURSDAY					
FRIDAY					
SATURDAY					
SUNDAY					
TOTAL HOURS					

NOTES : _____

_____

NAME: _____ WEEK: _____ MONTH: _____ YEAR: _____

DATE		TIME IN	TIME OUT	BREAKS	OVERTIME	TOTAL
MONDAY						
TUESDAY						
WEDNESDAY						
THURSDAY						
FRIDAY						
SATURDAY						
SUNDAY						
TOTAL HOURS						

NOTES : _____

_____

NAME: _____ WEEK: _____ MONTH: _____ YEAR: _____

DATE		TIME IN	TIME OUT	BREAKS	OVERTIME	TOTAL
MONDAY						
TUESDAY						
WEDNESDAY						
THURSDAY						
FRIDAY						
SATURDAY						
SUNDAY						
TOTAL HOURS						

NOTES : _____

_____

NAME: _____ WEEK: _____ MONTH: _____ YEAR: _____

DATE		TIME IN	TIME OUT	BREAKS	OVERTIME	TOTAL
MONDAY						
TUESDAY						
WEDNESDAY						
THURSDAY						
FRIDAY						
SATURDAY						
SUNDAY						
TOTAL HOURS						

NOTES : _____

_____

NAME: _____ WEEK: _____ MONTH: _____ YEAR: _____

DATE		TIME IN	TIME OUT	BREAKS	OVERTIME	TOTAL
MONDAY						
TUESDAY						
WEDNESDAY						
THURSDAY						
FRIDAY						
SATURDAY						
SUNDAY						
TOTAL HOURS						

NOTES : _____

_____

NAME: _____ WEEK: _____ MONTH: _____ YEAR: _____

DATE		TIME IN	TIME OUT	BREAKS	OVERTIME	TOTAL
MONDAY						
TUESDAY						
WEDNESDAY						
THURSDAY						
FRIDAY						
SATURDAY						
SUNDAY						
TOTAL HOURS						

NOTES : _____

_____

NAME: _____ WEEK: _____ MONTH: _____ YEAR: _____

DATE		TIME IN	TIME OUT	BREAKS	OVERTIME	TOTAL
MONDAY						
TUESDAY						
WEDNESDAY						
THURSDAY						
FRIDAY						
SATURDAY						
SUNDAY						
TOTAL HOURS						

NOTES : _____

_____

NAME: _____ WEEK: _____ MONTH: _____ YEAR: _____

DATE		TIME IN	TIME OUT	BREAKS	OVERTIME	TOTAL
MONDAY						
TUESDAY						
WEDNESDAY						
THURSDAY						
FRIDAY						
SATURDAY						
SUNDAY						
TOTAL HOURS						

NOTES : _____

_____

NAME: _____ WEEK: _____ MONTH: _____ YEAR: _____

DATE		TIME IN	TIME OUT	BREAKS	OVERTIME	TOTAL
MONDAY						
TUESDAY						
WEDNESDAY						
THURSDAY						
FRIDAY						
SATURDAY						
SUNDAY						
TOTAL HOURS						

NOTES : _____

_____

NAME: _____ WEEK: _____ MONTH: _____ YEAR: _____

DATE		TIME IN	TIME OUT	BREAKS	OVERTIME	TOTAL
MONDAY						
TUESDAY						
WEDNESDAY						
THURSDAY						
FRIDAY						
SATURDAY						
SUNDAY						
TOTAL HOURS						

NOTES : _____

_____

NAME: _____ WEEK: _____ MONTH: _____ YEAR: _____

DATE		TIME IN	TIME OUT	BREAKS	OVERTIME	TOTAL
MONDAY						
TUESDAY						
WEDNESDAY						
THURSDAY						
FRIDAY						
SATURDAY						
SUNDAY						
TOTAL HOURS						

NOTES : _____

_____

NAME: _____ WEEK: _____ MONTH: _____ YEAR: _____

DATE		TIME IN	TIME OUT	BREAKS	OVERTIME	TOTAL
MONDAY						
TUESDAY						
WEDNESDAY						
THURSDAY						
FRIDAY						
SATURDAY						
SUNDAY						
TOTAL HOURS						

NOTES : _____

_____

NAME: _____ WEEK: _____ MONTH: _____ YEAR: _____

DATE		TIME IN	TIME OUT	BREAKS	OVERTIME	TOTAL
MONDAY						
TUESDAY						
WEDNESDAY						
THURSDAY						
FRIDAY						
SATURDAY						
SUNDAY						
TOTAL HOURS						

NOTES : _____

_____

NAME: _____ WEEK: _____ MONTH: _____ YEAR: _____

DATE		TIME IN	TIME OUT	BREAKS	OVERTIME	TOTAL
MONDAY						
TUESDAY						
WEDNESDAY						
THURSDAY						
FRIDAY						
SATURDAY						
SUNDAY						
TOTAL HOURS						

NOTES : _____

_____

NAME: _____ WEEK: _____ MONTH: _____ YEAR: _____

DATE		TIME IN	TIME OUT	BREAKS	OVERTIME	TOTAL
MONDAY						
TUESDAY						
WEDNESDAY						
THURSDAY						
FRIDAY						
SATURDAY						
SUNDAY						
TOTAL HOURS						

NOTES : _____

_____

NAME: _____ WEEK: _____ MONTH: _____ YEAR: _____

DATE		TIME IN	TIME OUT	BREAKS	OVERTIME	TOTAL
MONDAY						
TUESDAY						
WEDNESDAY						
THURSDAY						
FRIDAY						
SATURDAY						
SUNDAY						
TOTAL HOURS						

NOTES : _____

_____

NAME: _____ WEEK: _____ MONTH: _____ YEAR: _____

DATE		TIME IN	TIME OUT	BREAKS	OVERTIME	TOTAL
MONDAY						
TUESDAY						
WEDNESDAY						
THURSDAY						
FRIDAY						
SATURDAY						
SUNDAY						
TOTAL HOURS						

NOTES : _____

_____

NAME: _____ WEEK: _____ MONTH: _____ YEAR: _____

DATE		TIME IN	TIME OUT	BREAKS	OVERTIME	TOTAL
MONDAY						
TUESDAY						
WEDNESDAY						
THURSDAY						
FRIDAY						
SATURDAY						
SUNDAY						
TOTAL HOURS						

NOTES : _____

_____

NAME: _____ WEEK: _____ MONTH: _____ YEAR: _____

DATE		TIME IN	TIME OUT	BREAKS	OVERTIME	TOTAL
MONDAY						
TUESDAY						
WEDNESDAY						
THURSDAY						
FRIDAY						
SATURDAY						
SUNDAY						
TOTAL HOURS						

NOTES : _____

_____

NAME: _____ WEEK: _____ MONTH: _____ YEAR: _____

DATE		TIME IN	TIME OUT	BREAKS	OVERTIME	TOTAL
MONDAY						
TUESDAY						
WEDNESDAY						
THURSDAY						
FRIDAY						
SATURDAY						
SUNDAY						
TOTAL HOURS						

NOTES : _____

_____

NAME: _____ WEEK: _____ MONTH: _____ YEAR: _____

DATE		TIME IN	TIME OUT	BREAKS	OVERTIME	TOTAL
MONDAY						
TUESDAY						
WEDNESDAY						
THURSDAY						
FRIDAY						
SATURDAY						
SUNDAY						
TOTAL HOURS						

NOTES : _____

_____

NAME: _____ WEEK: _____ MONTH: _____ YEAR: _____

DATE		TIME IN	TIME OUT	BREAKS	OVERTIME	TOTAL
MONDAY						
TUESDAY						
WEDNESDAY						
THURSDAY						
FRIDAY						
SATURDAY						
SUNDAY						
TOTAL HOURS						

NOTES : _____
_____

NAME: _____ WEEK: _____ MONTH: _____ YEAR: _____

DATE		TIME IN	TIME OUT	BREAKS	OVERTIME	TOTAL
MONDAY						
TUESDAY						
WEDNESDAY						
THURSDAY						
FRIDAY						
SATURDAY						
SUNDAY						
TOTAL HOURS						

NOTES : _____
_____

NAME: _____ WEEK: _____ MONTH: _____ YEAR: _____

DATE		TIME IN	TIME OUT	BREAKS	OVERTIME	TOTAL
MONDAY						
TUESDAY						
WEDNESDAY						
THURSDAY						
FRIDAY						
SATURDAY						
SUNDAY						
TOTAL HOURS						

NOTES : _____

_____

NAME: _____ WEEK: _____ MONTH: _____ YEAR: _____

DATE		TIME IN	TIME OUT	BREAKS	OVERTIME	TOTAL
MONDAY						
TUESDAY						
WEDNESDAY						
THURSDAY						
FRIDAY						
SATURDAY						
SUNDAY						
TOTAL HOURS						

NOTES : _____

_____

NAME: _____ WEEK: _____ MONTH: _____ YEAR: _____

DATE		TIME IN	TIME OUT	BREAKS	OVERTIME	TOTAL
MONDAY						
TUESDAY						
WEDNESDAY						
THURSDAY						
FRIDAY						
SATURDAY						
SUNDAY						
TOTAL HOURS						

NOTES : _____

_____

NAME: _____ WEEK: _____ MONTH: _____ YEAR: _____

DATE		TIME IN	TIME OUT	BREAKS	OVERTIME	TOTAL
MONDAY						
TUESDAY						
WEDNESDAY						
THURSDAY						
FRIDAY						
SATURDAY						
SUNDAY						
TOTAL HOURS						

NOTES : _____

_____

NAME: _____ WEEK: _____ MONTH: _____ YEAR: _____

DATE		TIME IN	TIME OUT	BREAKS	OVERTIME	TOTAL
MONDAY						
TUESDAY						
WEDNESDAY						
THURSDAY						
FRIDAY						
SATURDAY						
SUNDAY						
TOTAL HOURS						

NOTES : _____

_____

NAME: _____ WEEK: _____ MONTH: _____ YEAR: _____

DATE		TIME IN	TIME OUT	BREAKS	OVERTIME	TOTAL
MONDAY						
TUESDAY						
WEDNESDAY						
THURSDAY						
FRIDAY						
SATURDAY						
SUNDAY						
TOTAL HOURS						

NOTES : _____

_____

NAME: _____ WEEK: _____ MONTH: _____ YEAR: _____

DATE		TIME IN	TIME OUT	BREAKS	OVERTIME	TOTAL
MONDAY						
TUESDAY						
WEDNESDAY						
THURSDAY						
FRIDAY						
SATURDAY						
SUNDAY						
TOTAL HOURS						

NOTES : _____

_____

NAME: _____ WEEK: _____ MONTH: _____ YEAR: _____

DATE		TIME IN	TIME OUT	BREAKS	OVERTIME	TOTAL
MONDAY						
TUESDAY						
WEDNESDAY						
THURSDAY						
FRIDAY						
SATURDAY						
SUNDAY						
TOTAL HOURS						

NOTES : _____

_____

NAME: _____ WEEK: _____ MONTH: _____ YEAR: _____

DATE		TIME IN	TIME OUT	BREAKS	OVERTIME	TOTAL
MONDAY						
TUESDAY						
WEDNESDAY						
THURSDAY						
FRIDAY						
SATURDAY						
SUNDAY						
TOTAL HOURS						

NOTES : _____

_____

NAME: _____ WEEK: _____ MONTH: _____ YEAR: _____

DATE		TIME IN	TIME OUT	BREAKS	OVERTIME	TOTAL
MONDAY						
TUESDAY						
WEDNESDAY						
THURSDAY						
FRIDAY						
SATURDAY						
SUNDAY						
TOTAL HOURS						

NOTES : _____

_____

NAME: _____ WEEK: _____ MONTH: _____ YEAR: _____

DATE		TIME IN	TIME OUT	BREAKS	OVERTIME	TOTAL
MONDAY						
TUESDAY						
WEDNESDAY						
THURSDAY						
FRIDAY						
SATURDAY						
SUNDAY						
TOTAL HOURS						

NOTES : _____

_____

NAME: _____ WEEK: _____ MONTH: _____ YEAR: _____

DATE		TIME IN	TIME OUT	BREAKS	OVERTIME	TOTAL
MONDAY						
TUESDAY						
WEDNESDAY						
THURSDAY						
FRIDAY						
SATURDAY						
SUNDAY						
TOTAL HOURS						

NOTES : _____

_____

NAME: _____ WEEK: _____ MONTH: _____ YEAR: _____

DATE		TIME IN	TIME OUT	BREAKS	OVERTIME	TOTAL
MONDAY						
TUESDAY						
WEDNESDAY						
THURSDAY						
FRIDAY						
SATURDAY						
SUNDAY						
TOTAL HOURS						

NOTES : _____

_____

NAME: _____ WEEK: _____ MONTH: _____ YEAR: _____

DATE		TIME IN	TIME OUT	BREAKS	OVERTIME	TOTAL
MONDAY						
TUESDAY						
WEDNESDAY						
THURSDAY						
FRIDAY						
SATURDAY						
SUNDAY						
TOTAL HOURS						

NOTES : _____

_____

NAME: _____ WEEK: _____ MONTH: _____ YEAR: _____

DATE		TIME IN	TIME OUT	BREAKS	OVERTIME	TOTAL
MONDAY						
TUESDAY						
WEDNESDAY						
THURSDAY						
FRIDAY						
SATURDAY						
SUNDAY						
TOTAL HOURS						

NOTES : _____
_____

NAME: _____ WEEK: _____ MONTH: _____ YEAR: _____

DATE		TIME IN	TIME OUT	BREAKS	OVERTIME	TOTAL
MONDAY						
TUESDAY						
WEDNESDAY						
THURSDAY						
FRIDAY						
SATURDAY						
SUNDAY						
TOTAL HOURS						

NOTES : _____
_____

NAME: _____ **WEEK:** _____ **MONTH:** _____ **YEAR:** _____

DATE		TIME IN	TIME OUT	BREAKS	OVERTIME	TOTAL
MONDAY						
TUESDAY						
WEDNESDAY						
THURSDAY						
FRIDAY						
SATURDAY						
SUNDAY						
TOTAL HOURS						

NOTES : _____

_____

NAME: _____ **WEEK:** _____ **MONTH:** _____ **YEAR:** _____

DATE		TIME IN	TIME OUT	BREAKS	OVERTIME	TOTAL
MONDAY						
TUESDAY						
WEDNESDAY						
THURSDAY						
FRIDAY						
SATURDAY						
SUNDAY						
TOTAL HOURS						

NOTES : _____

_____

NAME: _____ WEEK: _____ MONTH: _____ YEAR: _____

DATE		TIME IN	TIME OUT	BREAKS	OVERTIME	TOTAL
MONDAY						
TUESDAY						
WEDNESDAY						
THURSDAY						
FRIDAY						
SATURDAY						
SUNDAY						
TOTAL HOURS						

NOTES : _____

_____

NAME: _____ WEEK: _____ MONTH: _____ YEAR: _____

DATE		TIME IN	TIME OUT	BREAKS	OVERTIME	TOTAL
MONDAY						
TUESDAY						
WEDNESDAY						
THURSDAY						
FRIDAY						
SATURDAY						
SUNDAY						
TOTAL HOURS						

NOTES : _____

_____

NAME: _____ WEEK: _____ MONTH: _____ YEAR: _____

DATE		TIME IN	TIME OUT	BREAKS	OVERTIME	TOTAL
MONDAY						
TUESDAY						
WEDNESDAY						
THURSDAY						
FRIDAY						
SATURDAY						
SUNDAY						
TOTAL HOURS						

NOTES : _____

_____

NAME: _____ WEEK: _____ MONTH: _____ YEAR: _____

DATE		TIME IN	TIME OUT	BREAKS	OVERTIME	TOTAL
MONDAY						
TUESDAY						
WEDNESDAY						
THURSDAY						
FRIDAY						
SATURDAY						
SUNDAY						
TOTAL HOURS						

NOTES : _____

_____

NAME: _____ WEEK: _____ MONTH: _____ YEAR: _____

DATE		TIME IN	TIME OUT	BREAKS	OVERTIME	TOTAL
MONDAY						
TUESDAY						
WEDNESDAY						
THURSDAY						
FRIDAY						
SATURDAY						
SUNDAY						
TOTAL HOURS						

NOTES : _____

_____

NAME: _____ WEEK: _____ MONTH: _____ YEAR: _____

DATE		TIME IN	TIME OUT	BREAKS	OVERTIME	TOTAL
MONDAY						
TUESDAY						
WEDNESDAY						
THURSDAY						
FRIDAY						
SATURDAY						
SUNDAY						
TOTAL HOURS						

NOTES : _____

_____

NAME: _____ WEEK: _____ MONTH: _____ YEAR: _____

DATE		TIME IN	TIME OUT	BREAKS	OVERTIME	TOTAL
MONDAY						
TUESDAY						
WEDNESDAY						
THURSDAY						
FRIDAY						
SATURDAY						
SUNDAY						
TOTAL HOURS						

NOTES : _____

_____

NAME: _____ WEEK: _____ MONTH: _____ YEAR: _____

DATE		TIME IN	TIME OUT	BREAKS	OVERTIME	TOTAL
MONDAY						
TUESDAY						
WEDNESDAY						
THURSDAY						
FRIDAY						
SATURDAY						
SUNDAY						
TOTAL HOURS						

NOTES : _____

_____

NAME: _____ WEEK: _____ MONTH: _____ YEAR: _____

DATE		TIME IN	TIME OUT	BREAKS	OVERTIME	TOTAL
MONDAY						
TUESDAY						
WEDNESDAY						
THURSDAY						
FRIDAY						
SATURDAY						
SUNDAY						
TOTAL HOURS						

NOTES : _____

_____

NAME: _____ WEEK: _____ MONTH: _____ YEAR: _____

DATE		TIME IN	TIME OUT	BREAKS	OVERTIME	TOTAL
MONDAY						
TUESDAY						
WEDNESDAY						
THURSDAY						
FRIDAY						
SATURDAY						
SUNDAY						
TOTAL HOURS						

NOTES : _____

_____

NAME: _____ WEEK: _____ MONTH: _____ YEAR: _____

DATE		TIME IN	TIME OUT	BREAKS	OVERTIME	TOTAL
MONDAY						
TUESDAY						
WEDNESDAY						
THURSDAY						
FRIDAY						
SATURDAY						
SUNDAY						
TOTAL HOURS						

NOTES : _____

_____

NAME: _____ WEEK: _____ MONTH: _____ YEAR: _____

DATE		TIME IN	TIME OUT	BREAKS	OVERTIME	TOTAL
MONDAY						
TUESDAY						
WEDNESDAY						
THURSDAY						
FRIDAY						
SATURDAY						
SUNDAY						
TOTAL HOURS						

NOTES : _____

_____

NAME: _____ WEEK: _____ MONTH: _____ YEAR: _____

DATE		TIME IN	TIME OUT	BREAKS	OVERTIME	TOTAL
MONDAY						
TUESDAY						
WEDNESDAY						
THURSDAY						
FRIDAY						
SATURDAY						
SUNDAY						
TOTAL HOURS						

NOTES : _____

_____

NAME: _____ WEEK: _____ MONTH: _____ YEAR: _____

DATE		TIME IN	TIME OUT	BREAKS	OVERTIME	TOTAL
MONDAY						
TUESDAY						
WEDNESDAY						
THURSDAY						
FRIDAY						
SATURDAY						
SUNDAY						
TOTAL HOURS						

NOTES : _____

_____

NAME: _____ WEEK: _____ MONTH: _____ YEAR: _____

DATE		TIME IN	TIME OUT	BREAKS	OVERTIME	TOTAL
MONDAY						
TUESDAY						
WEDNESDAY						
THURSDAY						
FRIDAY						
SATURDAY						
SUNDAY						
TOTAL HOURS						

NOTES : _____

_____

NAME: _____ WEEK: _____ MONTH: _____ YEAR: _____

DATE		TIME IN	TIME OUT	BREAKS	OVERTIME	TOTAL
MONDAY						
TUESDAY						
WEDNESDAY						
THURSDAY						
FRIDAY						
SATURDAY						
SUNDAY						
TOTAL HOURS						

NOTES : _____

_____

NAME: _____ WEEK: _____ MONTH: _____ YEAR: _____

DATE		TIME IN	TIME OUT	BREAKS	OVERTIME	TOTAL
MONDAY						
TUESDAY						
WEDNESDAY						
THURSDAY						
FRIDAY						
SATURDAY						
SUNDAY						
TOTAL HOURS						

NOTES : _____

_____

NAME: _____ WEEK: _____ MONTH: _____ YEAR: _____

DATE		TIME IN	TIME OUT	BREAKS	OVERTIME	TOTAL
MONDAY						
TUESDAY						
WEDNESDAY						
THURSDAY						
FRIDAY						
SATURDAY						
SUNDAY						
TOTAL HOURS						

NOTES : _____

_____

NAME: _____ WEEK: _____ MONTH: _____ YEAR: _____

DATE		TIME IN	TIME OUT	BREAKS	OVERTIME	TOTAL
MONDAY						
TUESDAY						
WEDNESDAY						
THURSDAY						
FRIDAY						
SATURDAY						
SUNDAY						
TOTAL HOURS						

NOTES : _____

_____

NAME: _____ WEEK: _____ MONTH: _____ YEAR: _____

DATE		TIME IN	TIME OUT	BREAKS	OVERTIME	TOTAL
MONDAY						
TUESDAY						
WEDNESDAY						
THURSDAY						
FRIDAY						
SATURDAY						
SUNDAY						
TOTAL HOURS						

NOTES : _____

_____

NAME: _____ WEEK: _____ MONTH: _____ YEAR: _____

DATE		TIME IN	TIME OUT	BREAKS	OVERTIME	TOTAL
MONDAY						
TUESDAY						
WEDNESDAY						
THURSDAY						
FRIDAY						
SATURDAY						
SUNDAY						
TOTAL HOURS						

NOTES : _____

_____

NAME: _____ WEEK: _____ MONTH: _____ YEAR: _____

DATE		TIME IN	TIME OUT	BREAKS	OVERTIME	TOTAL
MONDAY						
TUESDAY						
WEDNESDAY						
THURSDAY						
FRIDAY						
SATURDAY						
SUNDAY						
TOTAL HOURS						

NOTES : _____

_____

NAME: _____ WEEK: _____ MONTH: _____ YEAR: _____

DATE		TIME IN	TIME OUT	BREAKS	OVERTIME	TOTAL
MONDAY						
TUESDAY						
WEDNESDAY						
THURSDAY						
FRIDAY						
SATURDAY						
SUNDAY						
TOTAL HOURS						

NOTES : _____
_____

NAME: _____ WEEK: _____ MONTH: _____ YEAR: _____

DATE		TIME IN	TIME OUT	BREAKS	OVERTIME	TOTAL
MONDAY						
TUESDAY						
WEDNESDAY						
THURSDAY						
FRIDAY						
SATURDAY						
SUNDAY						
TOTAL HOURS						

NOTES : _____
_____

NAME: _____ WEEK: _____ MONTH: _____ YEAR: _____

DATE		TIME IN	TIME OUT	BREAKS	OVERTIME	TOTAL
MONDAY						
TUESDAY						
WEDNESDAY						
THURSDAY						
FRIDAY						
SATURDAY						
SUNDAY						
TOTAL HOURS						

NOTES : _____
_____

NAME: _____ WEEK: _____ MONTH: _____ YEAR: _____

DATE		TIME IN	TIME OUT	BREAKS	OVERTIME	TOTAL
MONDAY						
TUESDAY						
WEDNESDAY						
THURSDAY						
FRIDAY						
SATURDAY						
SUNDAY						
TOTAL HOURS						

NOTES : _____
_____

NAME: _____ WEEK: _____ MONTH: _____ YEAR: _____

DATE		TIME IN	TIME OUT	BREAKS	OVERTIME	TOTAL
MONDAY						
TUESDAY						
WEDNESDAY						
THURSDAY						
FRIDAY						
SATURDAY						
SUNDAY						
TOTAL HOURS						

NOTES : _____

_____

NAME: _____ WEEK: _____ MONTH: _____ YEAR: _____

DATE		TIME IN	TIME OUT	BREAKS	OVERTIME	TOTAL
MONDAY						
TUESDAY						
WEDNESDAY						
THURSDAY						
FRIDAY						
SATURDAY						
SUNDAY						
TOTAL HOURS						

NOTES : _____

_____

NAME: _____ WEEK: _____ MONTH: _____ YEAR: _____

DATE		TIME IN	TIME OUT	BREAKS	OVERTIME	TOTAL
MONDAY						
TUESDAY						
WEDNESDAY						
THURSDAY						
FRIDAY						
SATURDAY						
SUNDAY						
TOTAL HOURS						

NOTES : _____

_____

NAME: _____ WEEK: _____ MONTH: _____ YEAR: _____

DATE		TIME IN	TIME OUT	BREAKS	OVERTIME	TOTAL
MONDAY						
TUESDAY						
WEDNESDAY						
THURSDAY						
FRIDAY						
SATURDAY						
SUNDAY						
TOTAL HOURS						

NOTES : _____

_____

NAME: _____ WEEK: _____ MONTH: _____ YEAR: _____

DATE	TIME IN	TIME OUT	BREAKS	OVERTIME	TOTAL
MONDAY					
TUESDAY					
WEDNESDAY					
THURSDAY					
FRIDAY					
SATURDAY					
SUNDAY					
TOTAL HOURS					

NOTES : _____

_____

NAME: _____ WEEK: _____ MONTH: _____ YEAR: _____

DATE	TIME IN	TIME OUT	BREAKS	OVERTIME	TOTAL
MONDAY					
TUESDAY					
WEDNESDAY					
THURSDAY					
FRIDAY					
SATURDAY					
SUNDAY					
TOTAL HOURS					

NOTES : _____

_____

NAME: _____ WEEK: _____ MONTH: _____ YEAR: _____

DATE		TIME IN	TIME OUT	BREAKS	OVERTIME	TOTAL
MONDAY						
TUESDAY						
WEDNESDAY						
THURSDAY						
FRIDAY						
SATURDAY						
SUNDAY						
TOTAL HOURS						

NOTES : _____

_____

NAME: _____ WEEK: _____ MONTH: _____ YEAR: _____

DATE		TIME IN	TIME OUT	BREAKS	OVERTIME	TOTAL
MONDAY						
TUESDAY						
WEDNESDAY						
THURSDAY						
FRIDAY						
SATURDAY						
SUNDAY						
TOTAL HOURS						

NOTES : _____

_____

NAME: _____ WEEK: _____ MONTH: _____ YEAR: _____

DATE		TIME IN	TIME OUT	BREAKS	OVERTIME	TOTAL
MONDAY						
TUESDAY						
WEDNESDAY						
THURSDAY						
FRIDAY						
SATURDAY						
SUNDAY						
TOTAL HOURS						

NOTES : _____

_____

NAME: _____ WEEK: _____ MONTH: _____ YEAR: _____

DATE		TIME IN	TIME OUT	BREAKS	OVERTIME	TOTAL
MONDAY						
TUESDAY						
WEDNESDAY						
THURSDAY						
FRIDAY						
SATURDAY						
SUNDAY						
TOTAL HOURS						

NOTES : _____

_____

NAME: _____ WEEK: _____ MONTH: _____ YEAR: _____

DATE		TIME IN	TIME OUT	BREAKS	OVERTIME	TOTAL
MONDAY						
TUESDAY						
WEDNESDAY						
THURSDAY						
FRIDAY						
SATURDAY						
SUNDAY						
TOTAL HOURS						

NOTES : _____
_____

NAME: _____ WEEK: _____ MONTH: _____ YEAR: _____

DATE		TIME IN	TIME OUT	BREAKS	OVERTIME	TOTAL
MONDAY						
TUESDAY						
WEDNESDAY						
THURSDAY						
FRIDAY						
SATURDAY						
SUNDAY						
TOTAL HOURS						

NOTES : _____
_____

NAME: _____ WEEK: _____ MONTH: _____ YEAR: _____

DATE		TIME IN	TIME OUT	BREAKS	OVERTIME	TOTAL
MONDAY						
TUESDAY						
WEDNESDAY						
THURSDAY						
FRIDAY						
SATURDAY						
SUNDAY						
TOTAL HOURS						

NOTES : _____

_____

NAME: _____ WEEK: _____ MONTH: _____ YEAR: _____

DATE		TIME IN	TIME OUT	BREAKS	OVERTIME	TOTAL
MONDAY						
TUESDAY						
WEDNESDAY						
THURSDAY						
FRIDAY						
SATURDAY						
SUNDAY						
TOTAL HOURS						

NOTES : _____

_____

NAME: _____ WEEK: _____ MONTH: _____ YEAR: _____

DATE		TIME IN	TIME OUT	BREAKS	OVERTIME	TOTAL
MONDAY						
TUESDAY						
WEDNESDAY						
THURSDAY						
FRIDAY						
SATURDAY						
SUNDAY						
TOTAL HOURS						

NOTES : _____

_____

NAME: _____ WEEK: _____ MONTH: _____ YEAR: _____

DATE		TIME IN	TIME OUT	BREAKS	OVERTIME	TOTAL
MONDAY						
TUESDAY						
WEDNESDAY						
THURSDAY						
FRIDAY						
SATURDAY						
SUNDAY						
TOTAL HOURS						

NOTES : _____

_____

NAME: _____ WEEK: _____ MONTH: _____ YEAR: _____

DATE		TIME IN	TIME OUT	BREAKS	OVERTIME	TOTAL
MONDAY						
TUESDAY						
WEDNESDAY						
THURSDAY						
FRIDAY						
SATURDAY						
SUNDAY						
TOTAL HOURS						

NOTES : _____
_____

NAME: _____ WEEK: _____ MONTH: _____ YEAR: _____

DATE		TIME IN	TIME OUT	BREAKS	OVERTIME	TOTAL
MONDAY						
TUESDAY						
WEDNESDAY						
THURSDAY						
FRIDAY						
SATURDAY						
SUNDAY						
TOTAL HOURS						

NOTES : _____
_____

NAME: _____ WEEK: _____ MONTH: _____ YEAR: _____

DATE		TIME IN	TIME OUT	BREAKS	OVERTIME	TOTAL
MONDAY						
TUESDAY						
WEDNESDAY						
THURSDAY						
FRIDAY						
SATURDAY						
SUNDAY						
TOTAL HOURS						

NOTES : _____
_____

NAME: _____ WEEK: _____ MONTH: _____ YEAR: _____

DATE		TIME IN	TIME OUT	BREAKS	OVERTIME	TOTAL
MONDAY						
TUESDAY						
WEDNESDAY						
THURSDAY						
FRIDAY						
SATURDAY						
SUNDAY						
TOTAL HOURS						

NOTES : _____
_____

NAME: _____ WEEK: _____ MONTH: _____ YEAR: _____

DATE		TIME IN	TIME OUT	BREAKS	OVERTIME	TOTAL
MONDAY						
TUESDAY						
WEDNESDAY						
THURSDAY						
FRIDAY						
SATURDAY						
SUNDAY						
TOTAL HOURS						

NOTES : _____

_____

NAME: _____ WEEK: _____ MONTH: _____ YEAR: _____

DATE		TIME IN	TIME OUT	BREAKS	OVERTIME	TOTAL
MONDAY						
TUESDAY						
WEDNESDAY						
THURSDAY						
FRIDAY						
SATURDAY						
SUNDAY						
TOTAL HOURS						

NOTES : _____

_____

NAME: _____ WEEK: _____ MONTH: _____ YEAR: _____

DATE		TIME IN	TIME OUT	BREAKS	OVERTIME	TOTAL
MONDAY						
TUESDAY						
WEDNESDAY						
THURSDAY						
FRIDAY						
SATURDAY						
SUNDAY						
TOTAL HOURS						

NOTES : _____

_____

NAME: _____ WEEK: _____ MONTH: _____ YEAR: _____

DATE		TIME IN	TIME OUT	BREAKS	OVERTIME	TOTAL
MONDAY						
TUESDAY						
WEDNESDAY						
THURSDAY						
FRIDAY						
SATURDAY						
SUNDAY						
TOTAL HOURS						

NOTES : _____

_____

NAME: _____ WEEK: _____ MONTH: _____ YEAR: _____

DATE		TIME IN	TIME OUT	BREAKS	OVERTIME	TOTAL
MONDAY						
TUESDAY						
WEDNESDAY						
THURSDAY						
FRIDAY						
SATURDAY						
SUNDAY						
TOTAL HOURS						

NOTES : _____

_____

NAME: _____ WEEK: _____ MONTH: _____ YEAR: _____

DATE		TIME IN	TIME OUT	BREAKS	OVERTIME	TOTAL
MONDAY						
TUESDAY						
WEDNESDAY						
THURSDAY						
FRIDAY						
SATURDAY						
SUNDAY						
TOTAL HOURS						

NOTES : _____

_____

NAME: _____ WEEK: _____ MONTH: _____ YEAR: _____

DATE		TIME IN	TIME OUT	BREAKS	OVERTIME	TOTAL
MONDAY						
TUESDAY						
WEDNESDAY						
THURSDAY						
FRIDAY						
SATURDAY						
SUNDAY						
TOTAL HOURS						

NOTES : _____

_____

NAME: _____ WEEK: _____ MONTH: _____ YEAR: _____

DATE		TIME IN	TIME OUT	BREAKS	OVERTIME	TOTAL
MONDAY						
TUESDAY						
WEDNESDAY						
THURSDAY						
FRIDAY						
SATURDAY						
SUNDAY						
TOTAL HOURS						

NOTES : _____

_____

NAME: _____ WEEK: _____ MONTH: _____ YEAR: _____

DATE		TIME IN	TIME OUT	BREAKS	OVERTIME	TOTAL
MONDAY						
TUESDAY						
WEDNESDAY						
THURSDAY						
FRIDAY						
SATURDAY						
SUNDAY						
TOTAL HOURS						

NOTES : _____

_____

NAME: _____ WEEK: _____ MONTH: _____ YEAR: _____

DATE		TIME IN	TIME OUT	BREAKS	OVERTIME	TOTAL
MONDAY						
TUESDAY						
WEDNESDAY						
THURSDAY						
FRIDAY						
SATURDAY						
SUNDAY						
TOTAL HOURS						

NOTES : _____

_____

NAME: _____ WEEK: _____ MONTH: _____ YEAR: _____

DATE		TIME IN	TIME OUT	BREAKS	OVERTIME	TOTAL
MONDAY						
TUESDAY						
WEDNESDAY						
THURSDAY						
FRIDAY						
SATURDAY						
SUNDAY						
TOTAL HOURS						

NOTES : _____

_____

NAME: _____ WEEK: _____ MONTH: _____ YEAR: _____

DATE		TIME IN	TIME OUT	BREAKS	OVERTIME	TOTAL
MONDAY						
TUESDAY						
WEDNESDAY						
THURSDAY						
FRIDAY						
SATURDAY						
SUNDAY						
TOTAL HOURS						

NOTES : _____

_____

NAME: _____ WEEK: _____ MONTH: _____ YEAR: _____

DATE		TIME IN	TIME OUT	BREAKS	OVERTIME	TOTAL
MONDAY						
TUESDAY						
WEDNESDAY						
THURSDAY						
FRIDAY						
SATURDAY						
SUNDAY						
TOTAL HOURS						

NOTES : _____

_____

NAME: _____ WEEK: _____ MONTH: _____ YEAR: _____

DATE		TIME IN	TIME OUT	BREAKS	OVERTIME	TOTAL
MONDAY						
TUESDAY						
WEDNESDAY						
THURSDAY						
FRIDAY						
SATURDAY						
SUNDAY						
TOTAL HOURS						

NOTES : _____

_____

NAME: _____ WEEK: _____ MONTH: _____ YEAR: _____

DATE		TIME IN	TIME OUT	BREAKS	OVERTIME	TOTAL
MONDAY						
TUESDAY						
WEDNESDAY						
THURSDAY						
FRIDAY						
SATURDAY						
SUNDAY						
TOTAL HOURS						

NOTES : _____

_____

NAME: _____ WEEK: _____ MONTH: _____ YEAR: _____

DATE		TIME IN	TIME OUT	BREAKS	OVERTIME	TOTAL
MONDAY						
TUESDAY						
WEDNESDAY						
THURSDAY						
FRIDAY						
SATURDAY						
SUNDAY						
TOTAL HOURS						

NOTES : _____

_____

NAME: _____ WEEK: _____ MONTH: _____ YEAR: _____

DATE		TIME IN	TIME OUT	BREAKS	OVERTIME	TOTAL
MONDAY						
TUESDAY						
WEDNESDAY						
THURSDAY						
FRIDAY						
SATURDAY						
SUNDAY						
TOTAL HOURS						

NOTES : _____

_____

NAME: _____ WEEK: _____ MONTH: _____ YEAR: _____

DATE		TIME IN	TIME OUT	BREAKS	OVERTIME	TOTAL
MONDAY						
TUESDAY						
WEDNESDAY						
THURSDAY						
FRIDAY						
SATURDAY						
SUNDAY						
TOTAL HOURS						

NOTES : _____

_____

NAME: _____ WEEK: _____ MONTH: _____ YEAR: _____

DATE		TIME IN	TIME OUT	BREAKS	OVERTIME	TOTAL
MONDAY						
TUESDAY						
WEDNESDAY						
THURSDAY						
FRIDAY						
SATURDAY						
SUNDAY						
TOTAL HOURS						

NOTES : _____

_____

NAME: _____ WEEK: _____ MONTH: _____ YEAR: _____

DATE		TIME IN	TIME OUT	BREAKS	OVERTIME	TOTAL
MONDAY						
TUESDAY						
WEDNESDAY						
THURSDAY						
FRIDAY						
SATURDAY						
SUNDAY						
TOTAL HOURS						

NOTES : _____

_____

NAME: _____ WEEK: _____ MONTH: _____ YEAR: _____

DATE		TIME IN	TIME OUT	BREAKS	OVERTIME	TOTAL
MONDAY						
TUESDAY						
WEDNESDAY						
THURSDAY						
FRIDAY						
SATURDAY						
SUNDAY						
TOTAL HOURS						

NOTES : _____

_____

NAME: _____ WEEK: _____ MONTH: _____ YEAR: _____

DATE		TIME IN	TIME OUT	BREAKS	OVERTIME	TOTAL
MONDAY						
TUESDAY						
WEDNESDAY						
THURSDAY						
FRIDAY						
SATURDAY						
SUNDAY						
TOTAL HOURS						

NOTES : _____

_____

NAME: _____ WEEK: _____ MONTH: _____ YEAR: _____

DATE		TIME IN	TIME OUT	BREAKS	OVERTIME	TOTAL
MONDAY						
TUESDAY						
WEDNESDAY						
THURSDAY						
FRIDAY						
SATURDAY						
SUNDAY						
TOTAL HOURS						

NOTES : _____

_____

NAME: _____ WEEK: _____ MONTH: _____ YEAR: _____

DATE		TIME IN	TIME OUT	BREAKS	OVERTIME	TOTAL
MONDAY						
TUESDAY						
WEDNESDAY						
THURSDAY						
FRIDAY						
SATURDAY						
SUNDAY						
TOTAL HOURS						

NOTES : _____

_____

NAME: _____ WEEK: _____ MONTH: _____ YEAR: _____

DATE		TIME IN	TIME OUT	BREAKS	OVERTIME	TOTAL
MONDAY						
TUESDAY						
WEDNESDAY						
THURSDAY						
FRIDAY						
SATURDAY						
SUNDAY						
TOTAL HOURS						

NOTES : _____

_____

NAME: _____ WEEK: _____ MONTH: _____ YEAR: _____

DATE		TIME IN	TIME OUT	BREAKS	OVERTIME	TOTAL
MONDAY						
TUESDAY						
WEDNESDAY						
THURSDAY						
FRIDAY						
SATURDAY						
SUNDAY						
TOTAL HOURS						

NOTES : _____

_____

NAME: _____ WEEK: _____ MONTH: _____ YEAR: _____

DATE		TIME IN	TIME OUT	BREAKS	OVERTIME	TOTAL
MONDAY						
TUESDAY						
WEDNESDAY						
THURSDAY						
FRIDAY						
SATURDAY						
SUNDAY						
TOTAL HOURS						

NOTES : _____

_____

NAME: _____ WEEK: _____ MONTH: _____ YEAR: _____

DATE		TIME IN	TIME OUT	BREAKS	OVERTIME	TOTAL
MONDAY						
TUESDAY						
WEDNESDAY						
THURSDAY						
FRIDAY						
SATURDAY						
SUNDAY						
TOTAL HOURS						

NOTES : _____

_____

NAME: _____ WEEK: _____ MONTH: _____ YEAR: _____

DATE		TIME IN	TIME OUT	BREAKS	OVERTIME	TOTAL
MONDAY						
TUESDAY						
WEDNESDAY						
THURSDAY						
FRIDAY						
SATURDAY						
SUNDAY						
TOTAL HOURS						

NOTES : _____
_____

NAME: _____ WEEK: _____ MONTH: _____ YEAR: _____

DATE		TIME IN	TIME OUT	BREAKS	OVERTIME	TOTAL
MONDAY						
TUESDAY						
WEDNESDAY						
THURSDAY						
FRIDAY						
SATURDAY						
SUNDAY						
TOTAL HOURS						

NOTES : _____
_____

NAME: _____ WEEK: _____ MONTH: _____ YEAR: _____

DATE		TIME IN	TIME OUT	BREAKS	OVERTIME	TOTAL
MONDAY						
TUESDAY						
WEDNESDAY						
THURSDAY						
FRIDAY						
SATURDAY						
SUNDAY						
TOTAL HOURS						

NOTES : _____

_____

NAME: _____ WEEK: _____ MONTH: _____ YEAR: _____

DATE		TIME IN	TIME OUT	BREAKS	OVERTIME	TOTAL
MONDAY						
TUESDAY						
WEDNESDAY						
THURSDAY						
FRIDAY						
SATURDAY						
SUNDAY						
TOTAL HOURS						

NOTES : _____

_____

NAME: _____ WEEK: _____ MONTH: _____ YEAR: _____

DATE		TIME IN	TIME OUT	BREAKS	OVERTIME	TOTAL
MONDAY						
TUESDAY						
WEDNESDAY						
THURSDAY						
FRIDAY						
SATURDAY						
SUNDAY						
TOTAL HOURS						

NOTES : _____

_____

NAME: _____ WEEK: _____ MONTH: _____ YEAR: _____

DATE		TIME IN	TIME OUT	BREAKS	OVERTIME	TOTAL
MONDAY						
TUESDAY						
WEDNESDAY						
THURSDAY						
FRIDAY						
SATURDAY						
SUNDAY						
TOTAL HOURS						

NOTES : _____

_____

NAME: _____ WEEK: _____ MONTH: _____ YEAR: _____

DATE		TIME IN	TIME OUT	BREAKS	OVERTIME	TOTAL
MONDAY						
TUESDAY						
WEDNESDAY						
THURSDAY						
FRIDAY						
SATURDAY						
SUNDAY						
TOTAL HOURS						

NOTES : _____

_____

NAME: _____ WEEK: _____ MONTH: _____ YEAR: _____

DATE		TIME IN	TIME OUT	BREAKS	OVERTIME	TOTAL
MONDAY						
TUESDAY						
WEDNESDAY						
THURSDAY						
FRIDAY						
SATURDAY						
SUNDAY						
TOTAL HOURS						

NOTES : _____

_____

NAME: _____ WEEK: _____ MONTH: _____ YEAR: _____

DATE		TIME IN	TIME OUT	BREAKS	OVERTIME	TOTAL
MONDAY						
TUESDAY						
WEDNESDAY						
THURSDAY						
FRIDAY						
SATURDAY						
SUNDAY						
TOTAL HOURS						

NOTES : _____

_____

NAME: _____ WEEK: _____ MONTH: _____ YEAR: _____

DATE		TIME IN	TIME OUT	BREAKS	OVERTIME	TOTAL
MONDAY						
TUESDAY						
WEDNESDAY						
THURSDAY						
FRIDAY						
SATURDAY						
SUNDAY						
TOTAL HOURS						

NOTES : _____

_____

NAME: _____ WEEK: _____ MONTH: _____ YEAR: _____

DATE		TIME IN	TIME OUT	BREAKS	OVERTIME	TOTAL
MONDAY						
TUESDAY						
WEDNESDAY						
THURSDAY						
FRIDAY						
SATURDAY						
SUNDAY						
TOTAL HOURS						

NOTES : _____

_____

NAME: _____ WEEK: _____ MONTH: _____ YEAR: _____

DATE		TIME IN	TIME OUT	BREAKS	OVERTIME	TOTAL
MONDAY						
TUESDAY						
WEDNESDAY						
THURSDAY						
FRIDAY						
SATURDAY						
SUNDAY						
TOTAL HOURS						

NOTES : _____

_____

NAME: _____ WEEK: _____ MONTH: _____ YEAR: _____

DATE		TIME IN	TIME OUT	BREAKS	OVERTIME	TOTAL
MONDAY						
TUESDAY						
WEDNESDAY						
THURSDAY						
FRIDAY						
SATURDAY						
SUNDAY						
TOTAL HOURS						

NOTES : _____

_____

NAME: _____ WEEK: _____ MONTH: _____ YEAR: _____

DATE		TIME IN	TIME OUT	BREAKS	OVERTIME	TOTAL
MONDAY						
TUESDAY						
WEDNESDAY						
THURSDAY						
FRIDAY						
SATURDAY						
SUNDAY						
TOTAL HOURS						

NOTES : _____

_____

NAME: _____ WEEK: _____ MONTH: _____ YEAR: _____

DATE		TIME IN	TIME OUT	BREAKS	OVERTIME	TOTAL
MONDAY						
TUESDAY						
WEDNESDAY						
THURSDAY						
FRIDAY						
SATURDAY						
SUNDAY						
TOTAL HOURS						

NOTES : _____

_____

NAME: _____ WEEK: _____ MONTH: _____ YEAR: _____

DATE		TIME IN	TIME OUT	BREAKS	OVERTIME	TOTAL
MONDAY						
TUESDAY						
WEDNESDAY						
THURSDAY						
FRIDAY						
SATURDAY						
SUNDAY						
TOTAL HOURS						

NOTES : _____

_____

NAME: _____ WEEK: _____ MONTH: _____ YEAR: _____

DATE		TIME IN	TIME OUT	BREAKS	OVERTIME	TOTAL
MONDAY						
TUESDAY						
WEDNESDAY						
THURSDAY						
FRIDAY						
SATURDAY						
SUNDAY						
TOTAL HOURS						

NOTES : _____

_____

NAME: _____ WEEK: _____ MONTH: _____ YEAR: _____

DATE		TIME IN	TIME OUT	BREAKS	OVERTIME	TOTAL
MONDAY						
TUESDAY						
WEDNESDAY						
THURSDAY						
FRIDAY						
SATURDAY						
SUNDAY						
TOTAL HOURS						

NOTES : _____

_____

NAME: _____ WEEK: _____ MONTH: _____ YEAR: _____

DATE		TIME IN	TIME OUT	BREAKS	OVERTIME	TOTAL
MONDAY						
TUESDAY						
WEDNESDAY						
THURSDAY						
FRIDAY						
SATURDAY						
SUNDAY						
TOTAL HOURS						

NOTES : _____

_____

NAME: _____ WEEK: _____ MONTH: _____ YEAR: _____

DATE		TIME IN	TIME OUT	BREAKS	OVERTIME	TOTAL
MONDAY						
TUESDAY						
WEDNESDAY						
THURSDAY						
FRIDAY						
SATURDAY						
SUNDAY						
TOTAL HOURS						

NOTES : _____

_____

NAME: _____ WEEK: _____ MONTH: _____ YEAR: _____

DATE		TIME IN	TIME OUT	BREAKS	OVERTIME	TOTAL
MONDAY						
TUESDAY						
WEDNESDAY						
THURSDAY						
FRIDAY						
SATURDAY						
SUNDAY						
TOTAL HOURS						

NOTES : _____

_____

NAME: _____ WEEK: _____ MONTH: _____ YEAR: _____

DATE		TIME IN	TIME OUT	BREAKS	OVERTIME	TOTAL
MONDAY						
TUESDAY						
WEDNESDAY						
THURSDAY						
FRIDAY						
SATURDAY						
SUNDAY						
TOTAL HOURS						

NOTES : _____

_____

NAME: _____ WEEK: _____ MONTH: _____ YEAR: _____

DATE		TIME IN	TIME OUT	BREAKS	OVERTIME	TOTAL
MONDAY						
TUESDAY						
WEDNESDAY						
THURSDAY						
FRIDAY						
SATURDAY						
SUNDAY						
TOTAL HOURS						

NOTES : _____

_____

NAME: _____ WEEK: _____ MONTH: _____ YEAR: _____

DATE		TIME IN	TIME OUT	BREAKS	OVERTIME	TOTAL
MONDAY						
TUESDAY						
WEDNESDAY						
THURSDAY						
FRIDAY						
SATURDAY						
SUNDAY						
TOTAL HOURS						

NOTES : _____

_____

NAME: _____ WEEK: _____ MONTH: _____ YEAR: _____

DATE		TIME IN	TIME OUT	BREAKS	OVERTIME	TOTAL
MONDAY						
TUESDAY						
WEDNESDAY						
THURSDAY						
FRIDAY						
SATURDAY						
SUNDAY						
TOTAL HOURS						

NOTES : _____

_____

NAME: _____ WEEK: _____ MONTH: _____ YEAR: _____

DATE		TIME IN	TIME OUT	BREAKS	OVERTIME	TOTAL
MONDAY						
TUESDAY						
WEDNESDAY						
THURSDAY						
FRIDAY						
SATURDAY						
SUNDAY						
TOTAL HOURS						

NOTES : _____

_____

NAME: _____ WEEK: _____ MONTH: _____ YEAR: _____

DATE		TIME IN	TIME OUT	BREAKS	OVERTIME	TOTAL
MONDAY						
TUESDAY						
WEDNESDAY						
THURSDAY						
FRIDAY						
SATURDAY						
SUNDAY						
TOTAL HOURS						

NOTES : _____

_____

NAME: _____ WEEK: _____ MONTH: _____ YEAR: _____

DATE		TIME IN	TIME OUT	BREAKS	OVERTIME	TOTAL
MONDAY						
TUESDAY						
WEDNESDAY						
THURSDAY						
FRIDAY						
SATURDAY						
SUNDAY						
TOTAL HOURS						

NOTES : _____

_____

NAME: _____ WEEK: _____ MONTH: _____ YEAR: _____

DATE		TIME IN	TIME OUT	BREAKS	OVERTIME	TOTAL
MONDAY						
TUESDAY						
WEDNESDAY						
THURSDAY						
FRIDAY						
SATURDAY						
SUNDAY						
TOTAL HOURS						

NOTES : _____

_____

NAME: _____ WEEK: _____ MONTH: _____ YEAR: _____

DATE		TIME IN	TIME OUT	BREAKS	OVERTIME	TOTAL
MONDAY						
TUESDAY						
WEDNESDAY						
THURSDAY						
FRIDAY						
SATURDAY						
SUNDAY						
TOTAL HOURS						

NOTES : _____

_____

NAME: _____ WEEK: _____ MONTH: _____ YEAR: _____

DATE		TIME IN	TIME OUT	BREAKS	OVERTIME	TOTAL
MONDAY						
TUESDAY						
WEDNESDAY						
THURSDAY						
FRIDAY						
SATURDAY						
SUNDAY						
TOTAL HOURS						

NOTES : _____

_____

NAME: _____ WEEK: _____ MONTH: _____ YEAR: _____

DATE		TIME IN	TIME OUT	BREAKS	OVERTIME	TOTAL
MONDAY						
TUESDAY						
WEDNESDAY						
THURSDAY						
FRIDAY						
SATURDAY						
SUNDAY						
TOTAL HOURS						

NOTES : _____

_____

NAME: _____ WEEK: _____ MONTH: _____ YEAR: _____

DATE		TIME IN	TIME OUT	BREAKS	OVERTIME	TOTAL
MONDAY						
TUESDAY						
WEDNESDAY						
THURSDAY						
FRIDAY						
SATURDAY						
SUNDAY						
TOTAL HOURS						

NOTES : _____

_____

NAME: _____ WEEK: _____ MONTH: _____ YEAR: _____

DATE		TIME IN	TIME OUT	BREAKS	OVERTIME	TOTAL
MONDAY						
TUESDAY						
WEDNESDAY						
THURSDAY						
FRIDAY						
SATURDAY						
SUNDAY						
TOTAL HOURS						

NOTES : _____

_____

NAME: _____ WEEK: _____ MONTH: _____ YEAR: _____

DATE		TIME IN	TIME OUT	BREAKS	OVERTIME	TOTAL
MONDAY						
TUESDAY						
WEDNESDAY						
THURSDAY						
FRIDAY						
SATURDAY						
SUNDAY						
TOTAL HOURS						

NOTES : _____
_____

NAME: _____ WEEK: _____ MONTH: _____ YEAR: _____

DATE		TIME IN	TIME OUT	BREAKS	OVERTIME	TOTAL
MONDAY						
TUESDAY						
WEDNESDAY						
THURSDAY						
FRIDAY						
SATURDAY						
SUNDAY						
TOTAL HOURS						

NOTES : _____
_____

NAME: _____ WEEK: _____ MONTH: _____ YEAR: _____

DATE		TIME IN	TIME OUT	BREAKS	OVERTIME	TOTAL
MONDAY						
TUESDAY						
WEDNESDAY						
THURSDAY						
FRIDAY						
SATURDAY						
SUNDAY						
TOTAL HOURS						

NOTES : _____

_____

NAME: _____ WEEK: _____ MONTH: _____ YEAR: _____

DATE		TIME IN	TIME OUT	BREAKS	OVERTIME	TOTAL
MONDAY						
TUESDAY						
WEDNESDAY						
THURSDAY						
FRIDAY						
SATURDAY						
SUNDAY						
TOTAL HOURS						

NOTES : _____

_____

NAME: _____ WEEK: _____ MONTH: _____ YEAR: _____

DATE		TIME IN	TIME OUT	BREAKS	OVERTIME	TOTAL
MONDAY						
TUESDAY						
WEDNESDAY						
THURSDAY						
FRIDAY						
SATURDAY						
SUNDAY						
TOTAL HOURS						

NOTES : _____

_____

NAME: _____ WEEK: _____ MONTH: _____ YEAR: _____

DATE		TIME IN	TIME OUT	BREAKS	OVERTIME	TOTAL
MONDAY						
TUESDAY						
WEDNESDAY						
THURSDAY						
FRIDAY						
SATURDAY						
SUNDAY						
TOTAL HOURS						

NOTES : _____

_____

NAME: _____ WEEK: _____ MONTH: _____ YEAR: _____

DATE		TIME IN	TIME OUT	BREAKS	OVERTIME	TOTAL
MONDAY						
TUESDAY						
WEDNESDAY						
THURSDAY						
FRIDAY						
SATURDAY						
SUNDAY						
TOTAL HOURS						

NOTES : _____

_____

NAME: _____ WEEK: _____ MONTH: _____ YEAR: _____

DATE		TIME IN	TIME OUT	BREAKS	OVERTIME	TOTAL
MONDAY						
TUESDAY						
WEDNESDAY						
THURSDAY						
FRIDAY						
SATURDAY						
SUNDAY						
TOTAL HOURS						

NOTES : _____

_____

NAME: _____ WEEK: _____ MONTH: _____ YEAR: _____

DATE		TIME IN	TIME OUT	BREAKS	OVERTIME	TOTAL
MONDAY						
TUESDAY						
WEDNESDAY						
THURSDAY						
FRIDAY						
SATURDAY						
SUNDAY						
TOTAL HOURS						

NOTES : _____

_____

NAME: _____ WEEK: _____ MONTH: _____ YEAR: _____

DATE		TIME IN	TIME OUT	BREAKS	OVERTIME	TOTAL
MONDAY						
TUESDAY						
WEDNESDAY						
THURSDAY						
FRIDAY						
SATURDAY						
SUNDAY						
TOTAL HOURS						

NOTES : _____

_____

NAME: _____ WEEK: _____ MONTH: _____ YEAR: _____

DATE	TIME IN	TIME OUT	BREAKS	OVERTIME	TOTAL
MONDAY					
TUESDAY					
WEDNESDAY					
THURSDAY					
FRIDAY					
SATURDAY					
SUNDAY					
TOTAL HOURS					

NOTES : _____

_____

NAME: _____ WEEK: _____ MONTH: _____ YEAR: _____

DATE	TIME IN	TIME OUT	BREAKS	OVERTIME	TOTAL
MONDAY					
TUESDAY					
WEDNESDAY					
THURSDAY					
FRIDAY					
SATURDAY					
SUNDAY					
TOTAL HOURS					

NOTES : _____

_____

NAME: _____ WEEK: _____ MONTH: _____ YEAR: _____

DATE		TIME IN	TIME OUT	BREAKS	OVERTIME	TOTAL
MONDAY						
TUESDAY						
WEDNESDAY						
THURSDAY						
FRIDAY						
SATURDAY						
SUNDAY						
TOTAL HOURS						

NOTES : _____

_____

NAME: _____ WEEK: _____ MONTH: _____ YEAR: _____

DATE		TIME IN	TIME OUT	BREAKS	OVERTIME	TOTAL
MONDAY						
TUESDAY						
WEDNESDAY						
THURSDAY						
FRIDAY						
SATURDAY						
SUNDAY						
TOTAL HOURS						

NOTES : _____

_____

NAME: _____ WEEK: _____ MONTH: _____ YEAR: _____

DATE		TIME IN	TIME OUT	BREAKS	OVERTIME	TOTAL
MONDAY						
TUESDAY						
WEDNESDAY						
THURSDAY						
FRIDAY						
SATURDAY						
SUNDAY						
TOTAL HOURS						

NOTES : _____

_____

NAME: _____ WEEK: _____ MONTH: _____ YEAR: _____

DATE		TIME IN	TIME OUT	BREAKS	OVERTIME	TOTAL
MONDAY						
TUESDAY						
WEDNESDAY						
THURSDAY						
FRIDAY						
SATURDAY						
SUNDAY						
TOTAL HOURS						

NOTES : _____

_____

NAME: _____ WEEK: _____ MONTH: _____ YEAR: _____

DATE		TIME IN	TIME OUT	BREAKS	OVERTIME	TOTAL
MONDAY						
TUESDAY						
WEDNESDAY						
THURSDAY						
FRIDAY						
SATURDAY						
SUNDAY						
TOTAL HOURS						

NOTES : _____

_____

NAME: _____ WEEK: _____ MONTH: _____ YEAR: _____

DATE		TIME IN	TIME OUT	BREAKS	OVERTIME	TOTAL
MONDAY						
TUESDAY						
WEDNESDAY						
THURSDAY						
FRIDAY						
SATURDAY						
SUNDAY						
TOTAL HOURS						

NOTES : _____

_____

NAME: _____ WEEK: _____ MONTH: _____ YEAR: _____

DATE		TIME IN	TIME OUT	BREAKS	OVERTIME	TOTAL
MONDAY						
TUESDAY						
WEDNESDAY						
THURSDAY						
FRIDAY						
SATURDAY						
SUNDAY						
TOTAL HOURS						

NOTES : _____

_____

NAME: _____ WEEK: _____ MONTH: _____ YEAR: _____

DATE		TIME IN	TIME OUT	BREAKS	OVERTIME	TOTAL
MONDAY						
TUESDAY						
WEDNESDAY						
THURSDAY						
FRIDAY						
SATURDAY						
SUNDAY						
TOTAL HOURS						

NOTES : _____

_____

NAME: _____ WEEK: _____ MONTH: _____ YEAR: _____

DATE		TIME IN	TIME OUT	BREAKS	OVERTIME	TOTAL
MONDAY						
TUESDAY						
WEDNESDAY						
THURSDAY						
FRIDAY						
SATURDAY						
SUNDAY						
TOTAL HOURS						

NOTES : _____

_____

NAME: _____ WEEK: _____ MONTH: _____ YEAR: _____

DATE		TIME IN	TIME OUT	BREAKS	OVERTIME	TOTAL
MONDAY						
TUESDAY						
WEDNESDAY						
THURSDAY						
FRIDAY						
SATURDAY						
SUNDAY						
TOTAL HOURS						

NOTES : _____

_____

NAME: _____ WEEK: _____ MONTH: _____ YEAR: _____

DATE		TIME IN	TIME OUT	BREAKS	OVERTIME	TOTAL
MONDAY						
TUESDAY						
WEDNESDAY						
THURSDAY						
FRIDAY						
SATURDAY						
SUNDAY						
TOTAL HOURS						

NOTES : _____

_____

NAME: _____ WEEK: _____ MONTH: _____ YEAR: _____

DATE		TIME IN	TIME OUT	BREAKS	OVERTIME	TOTAL
MONDAY						
TUESDAY						
WEDNESDAY						
THURSDAY						
FRIDAY						
SATURDAY						
SUNDAY						
TOTAL HOURS						

NOTES : _____

_____

NAME: _____ WEEK: _____ MONTH: _____ YEAR: _____

DATE		TIME IN	TIME OUT	BREAKS	OVERTIME	TOTAL
MONDAY						
TUESDAY						
WEDNESDAY						
THURSDAY						
FRIDAY						
SATURDAY						
SUNDAY						
TOTAL HOURS						

NOTES : _____

_____

NAME: _____ WEEK: _____ MONTH: _____ YEAR: _____

DATE		TIME IN	TIME OUT	BREAKS	OVERTIME	TOTAL
MONDAY						
TUESDAY						
WEDNESDAY						
THURSDAY						
FRIDAY						
SATURDAY						
SUNDAY						
TOTAL HOURS						

NOTES : _____

_____

NAME: _____ WEEK: _____ MONTH: _____ YEAR: _____

DATE	TIME IN	TIME OUT	BREAKS	OVERTIME	TOTAL
MONDAY					
TUESDAY					
WEDNESDAY					
THURSDAY					
FRIDAY					
SATURDAY					
SUNDAY					
TOTAL HOURS					

NOTES : _____
_____

NAME: _____ WEEK: _____ MONTH: _____ YEAR: _____

DATE	TIME IN	TIME OUT	BREAKS	OVERTIME	TOTAL
MONDAY					
TUESDAY					
WEDNESDAY					
THURSDAY					
FRIDAY					
SATURDAY					
SUNDAY					
TOTAL HOURS					

NOTES : _____
_____

NAME: _____ WEEK: _____ MONTH: _____ YEAR: _____

DATE		TIME IN	TIME OUT	BREAKS	OVERTIME	TOTAL
MONDAY						
TUESDAY						
WEDNESDAY						
THURSDAY						
FRIDAY						
SATURDAY						
SUNDAY						
TOTAL HOURS						

NOTES : _____

_____

NAME: _____ WEEK: _____ MONTH: _____ YEAR: _____

DATE		TIME IN	TIME OUT	BREAKS	OVERTIME	TOTAL
MONDAY						
TUESDAY						
WEDNESDAY						
THURSDAY						
FRIDAY						
SATURDAY						
SUNDAY						
TOTAL HOURS						

NOTES : _____

_____

NAME: _____ **WEEK:** _____ **MONTH:** _____ **YEAR:** _____

DATE		TIME IN	TIME OUT	BREAKS	OVERTIME	TOTAL
MONDAY						
TUESDAY						
WEDNESDAY						
THURSDAY						
FRIDAY						
SATURDAY						
SUNDAY						
TOTAL HOURS						

NOTES : _____

_____

NAME: _____ **WEEK:** _____ **MONTH:** _____ **YEAR:** _____

DATE		TIME IN	TIME OUT	BREAKS	OVERTIME	TOTAL
MONDAY						
TUESDAY						
WEDNESDAY						
THURSDAY						
FRIDAY						
SATURDAY						
SUNDAY						
TOTAL HOURS						

NOTES : _____

_____

NAME: _____ WEEK: _____ MONTH: _____ YEAR: _____

DATE		TIME IN	TIME OUT	BREAKS	OVERTIME	TOTAL
MONDAY						
TUESDAY						
WEDNESDAY						
THURSDAY						
FRIDAY						
SATURDAY						
SUNDAY						
TOTAL HOURS						

NOTES : _____

_____

NAME: _____ WEEK: _____ MONTH: _____ YEAR: _____

DATE		TIME IN	TIME OUT	BREAKS	OVERTIME	TOTAL
MONDAY						
TUESDAY						
WEDNESDAY						
THURSDAY						
FRIDAY						
SATURDAY						
SUNDAY						
TOTAL HOURS						

NOTES : _____

_____

www.ingramcontent.com/pod-product-compliance
Lightning Source LLC
Chambersburg PA
CBHW081821200326
41597CB00023B/4343